THE SPECTACULAR SCIENCE of INVENTIONS

written by
Rob Colson

illustrated by
Moreno
Chiacchiera

KINGFISHER

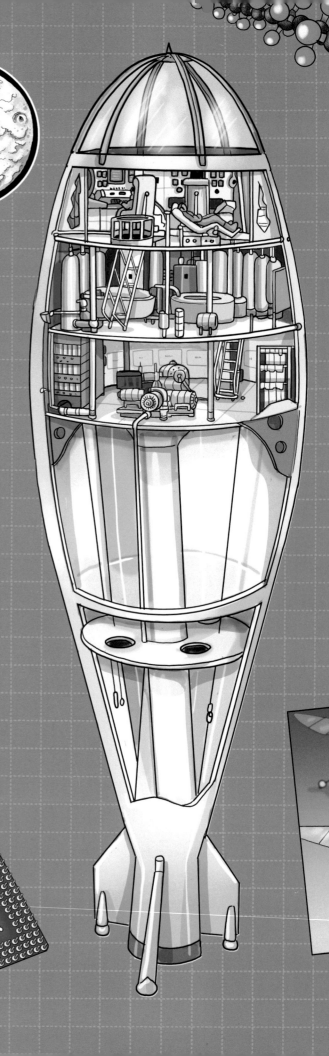

KINGFISHER
LONDON & NEW YORK

First published 2024 in the United States
by Kingfisher
120 Broadway, New York, NY 10271
Kingfisher is an imprint of
Macmillan Children's Books, London

ISBN 978-0-7534-7963-6

Distributed in the U.S. and Canada by Macmillan,
120 Broadway, New York, NY 10271

Library of Congress Cataloging-in-Publication
data has been applied for.

Author: Rob Colson
Illustrator: Moreno Chiacchiera
Consultant: Penny Johnson
Designed and edited by Tall Tree Ltd

Kingfisher Books are available for special
promotions and premiums.
For details contact:
Special Markets Department, Macmillan
120 Broadway, New York, NY 10271.

For more information please visit:
www.kingfisherbooks.com

Printed in China
2 4 6 8 9 7 5 3 1
1TR/0224/WKT/RV/128MA

EU representative:
1st Floor, The Liffey Trust Centre
117-126 Sheriff Street Upper,
Dublin 1 D01 YC43

CONTENTS

A WORLD OF INVENTION

People have been creating new inventions for thousands of years. Today, we are surrounded by all kinds of designs that make our lives easier, and scientists and engineers around the world are hard at work creating the amazing inventions of tomorrow.

AHEAD OF HIS TIME

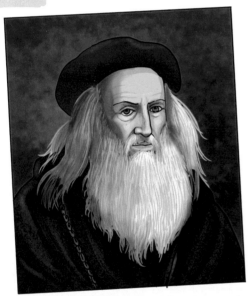

Leonardo da Vinci

Some inventors come up with ideas that are impossible to build in their own lifetimes. Italian artist and engineer Leonardo da Vinci (1452–1519) produced designs for inventions that would only be made much later. These included a helicopter, a parachute, an armored tank, and shoes made of cork for walking on water.

Parachute

Tank

Helicopter

Walking on water

MAKING A DIFFERENCE

American inventor George Washington Carver (c.1864–1943) developed hundreds of new ideas in his research at Tuskegee University, Alabama. Carver taught farmers new ways to improve the soil on their farms. In 1906, he made the Jesup Agricultural Wagon, a mobile classroom that he drove from farm to farm teaching soil chemistry.

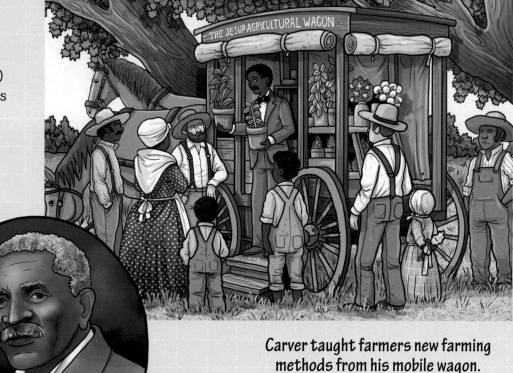

George Washington Carver

Carver taught farmers new farming methods from his mobile wagon.

Protecting your idea

Inventors protect their new ideas by taking out a patent. A patent is a legal document that grants the inventor the sole right to make their invention for a fixed period of time.

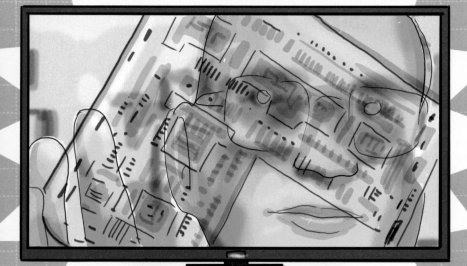

WORLD'S MOST PROLIFIC INVENTOR

Japanese inventor Shunpei Yamazaki (born 1942) has filed more than 11,000 patents. His inventions include the thin-film transistor, an electronic device used in the LCD display screens of flat-screen TVs.

ANCIENT INVENTIONS

We do not know who thought up the first inventions, but ancient remains show us that humans have been creating new tools and gadgets for hundreds of thousands of years.

The oldest tools date back more than 2 million years to ancestors of modern humans such as *Homo habilis*. They made their tools by smashing stones against one another. The sharpened edge was used for cutting and sawing.

Early stone tools were roughly the same size as a computer mouse, as they were made to fit comfortably in the palm of the hand.

MAMMOTH HUNT

Fully modern humans appeared on Earth about 200,000 years ago. By this time, stone tool technology had become more sophisticated. The toolkit included axes, spears, and scrapers. People used these tools to hunt large animals such as mammoths.

INVENTING THE WHEEL

The wheel was invented several times by different groups of people. Some of the earliest wheeled vehicles were made by the Sumerians in ancient Mesopotamia (modern-day Iraq) around 3500 BCE. These were wheeled wagons or chariots.

Early wheels were made of wood.

This four-wheeled war chariot is depicted on a Sumerian wooden box called the Standard of Ur. It was pulled by a team of four onagers (a kind of wild donkey).

DRINKING CHOCOLATE

Chocolate was invented in Mesoamerica around 4,000 years ago. Made from a preparation of beans from the cacao tree, chocolate was prepared as a drink flavored with chilis. When Europeans arrived in the Americas in the 16th century, they found the drink too bitter and added sugar to it. Solid chocolate bars were invented in the 19th century.

The Aztecs of Mesoamerica made their chocolate drink frothy by pouring it from one vessel into another.

WRITING

The first writing systems were invented more than 5,000 years ago. The invention of writing allowed people to make permanent records, passing on knowledge to future generations.

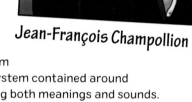

Writing in clay

The earliest known writing was invented in about 3400 BCE by the Sumerians in Mesopotamia. Called cuneiform, it was made up of a series of wedge-shaped marks made in clay. Thousands of tablets have survived from the time, recording details of family life and business deals.

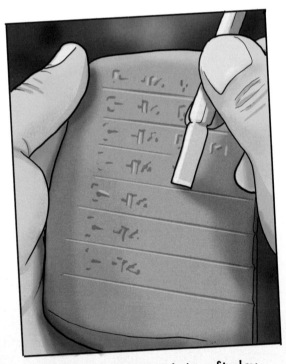

Wedge marks were made in soft clay, which hardened when it dried.

Hieroglyphs

Around 3000 BCE, the ancient Egyptians developed a writing system called hieroglyphs. This system contained around 1,000 symbols representing both meanings and sounds. Our understanding of hieroglyphs was lost for more than 1,000 years until the Rosetta Stone was discovered in Egypt in 1799. It contained a decree issued by pharaoh Ptolemy V in 196 BCE, with the same words written in Greek, Egyptian hieroglyphs and an Egyptian script called Demotic. In 1822, French linguist Jean-François Champollion (1790–1832) deciphered the meaning of the hieroglyphs by comparing the three texts.

Jean-François Champollion

On the Rosetta stone, the name of the pharaoh Ptolemy appears in hieroglyphs, Demotic, and Greek.

Rosetta stone

Hieroglyph

Demotic

Greek

Chinese characters

Chinese characters were first developed just over 3,000 years ago, which makes Chinese the oldest writing system still in use today. It uses thousands of different characters representing a word or a syllable (part of a word). Today, Chinese characters are also used to write languages such as Japanese.

木	人	雨	田
Tree	Person	Rain	Field

Petrache Poenaru

Fountain pen

The ancient Egyptians wrote using thick reeds, while the ancient Chinese used brushes. Later, a feather quill was commonly used. All of these writing tools needed to be dipped in ink. In 1827, Romanian inventor Petrache Poenaru (1799–1875) invented the fountain pen, the first pen that carried its own ink.

Ink flows into the nib from a tank behind it.

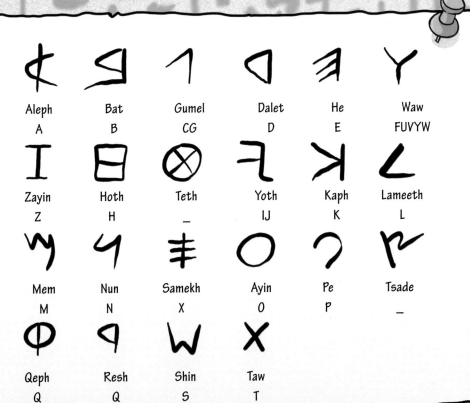

Phoenician alphabet

Instead of representing meanings, an alphabet records only the sounds made by a language. This allows the language to be written using far fewer symbols. The first alphabet was invented about 3,000 years ago by the ancient Phoenicians (who lived in modern-day Lebanon). Their alphabet contained 22 symbols, each representing a different consonant sound. Today, more than 100 different alphabets are in use around the world.

Aleph	Bat	Gumel	Dalet	He	Waw
A	B	CG	D	E	FUVYW

Zayin	Hoth	Teth	Yoth	Kaph	Lameeth
Z	H	–	IJ	K	L

Mem	Nun	Samekh	Ayin	Pe	Tsade
M	N	X	O	P	–

Qeph	Resh	Shin	Taw
Q	Q	S	T

THE PRINTING PRESS

The invention of the printing press allowed text to be mass-produced for the first time. Printing presses using movable blocks with letters or characters on them were first developed in China and Korea and later spread across the world.

Writing by hand

Before the printing press, books had to be written by hand. In Medieval Europe, teams of monks copied religious texts to produce lavish books called illuminated manuscripts, which were a mix of writing and drawings. The monks would often draw mythical creatures in the margins.

FIRST PRINTERS

Nobody knows who invented the printing press, but the first mass-produced book was printed by Chinese inventor Wang Zhen in 1313. The book is called *Nong Shu (Book of Agriculture)*. It covers a wide variety of topics, including the system of movable wooden blocks that Zhen had used to print the book.

Printers arranged wooden blocks with Chinese characters carved into them on revolving plates.

PRINTING THE BIBLE

In the 15th century, German inventor Johannes Gutenberg introduced the printing press to Europe. Gutenberg used metal blocks for the letters. The blocks were manufactured using molds, which made the letters uniform in size and shape. In 1455, Gutenberg produced the first printed version of the Christian Bible.

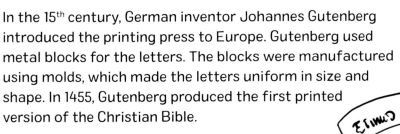

Face

Shoulder

Groove

Body

Point size
(size of letter)

Nick
(helps position
the letter)

Setting type
A typesetter arranges the type in rows in a tray called a composing stick. The rows are transferred to a larger tray called a galley, which contains whole pages for printing. The book is printed by spreading ink over the galley and pressing a piece of paper over it.

SPREADING THE WRITTEN WORD

Gutenberg's printing methods quickly spread across Europe and the world, allowing knowledge to spread more quickly than ever before. The first weekly newspapers were printed in Germany in 1609. By the 19th century, high-speed steam-powered presses allowed the printing of daily newspapers, creating the first mass media with the written word made available to everyone. Today, most printing is done digitally and printing presses are no longer set by hand.

"Read all about it!"

In the 19th century, children sold newspapers in the streets.

11

INVENTIONS OF THE HAN DYNASTY

The Han Dynasty in China lasted from 206 BCE to 220 CE. This 400-year period saw a flowering of new ideas in art and science, and a number of important new inventions.

COMPASS

The magnetic compass was invented about 2,000 years ago. It used a spoon made from a naturally occurring mineral called lodestone, or magnetite. The spoon was balanced on a bronze plate, and the handle would move to point to the south. Early compasses were very delicate and not practical for navigation. They were used to calculate the best angle to place buildings or even to divine future events.

The spoon was placed on a "heaven board" on which the constellations were marked.

Handle points south.

Portable magnet

By 700 CE, Chinese scientists had worked out a way to magnetize an iron needle by stroking it with magnetite. Suspended from a silk thread or floating in water, the needle would line up north to south. This invention allowed the first practical compasses to be developed for navigation. From about 1000 CE, Chinese trading ships carried portable compasses to help them find their way.

You can make a simple compass at home by floating a magnetized needle on a piece of cork.

RUDDER

From the first century CE, Chinese boats were fitted with rudders. This invention allowed sailors to steer ships much more easily.

The rudder was controlled by a lever.

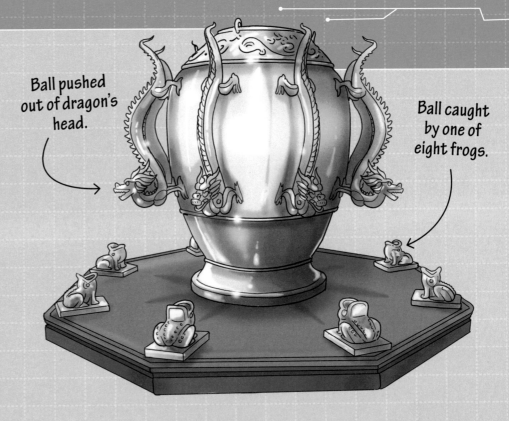

Ball pushed out of dragon's head.

Ball caught by one of eight frogs.

DETECTING EARTHQUAKES

Chinese astronomer Zhang Heng (78–139 CE) invented a device to detect distant earthquakes. Zhang's seismograph was an urn with a pendulum inside it. When it picked up a vibration, the pendulum pushed a ball into the mouth of one of eight frogs surrounding the urn. The location of the frog showed the direction the earthquake had come from.

PAPER

The invention of paper is traditionally credited to court official Cai Lun (died 121 CE). Although he probably did not invent paper, Cai Lun did produce the first reliable recipe for its manufacture, using a pulp made from tree bark, cloth rags, and old nets. The pulp was combined with water, flattened, and dried, then cut into sheets. Writing on paper became widespread in China over the following centuries.

1 Wood, bark, and cloth are soaked to make a pulp.

2 Pulp is flattened and dried.

3 The paper is cut into sheets.

MAKING METALS

Metals such as copper and iron were first used to make tools about 10,000 years ago. However, these metals needed to be mixed with other substances to make them really useful.

BRONZE

Bronze was invented about 7,000 years ago. It is an alloy (mix) of copper with small amounts of tin. The copper and tin are melted together by heating them to over 1,800°F. While the bronze is molten, it can be cast into different shapes before it cools and hardens. Bronze is much harder than copper, and for the first time, objects such as tools and weapons could be made from metal rather than stone.

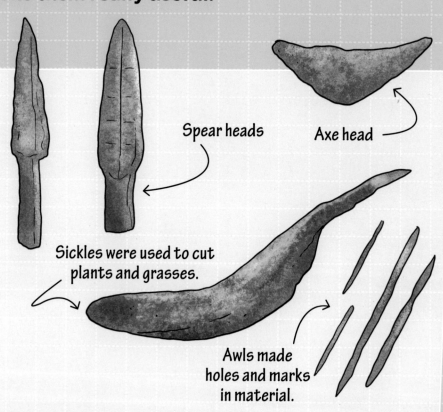

Spear heads

Axe head

Sickles were used to cut plants and grasses.

Awls made holes and marks in material.

STEEL

Steel is an alloy of iron and small amounts of carbon and sometimes other substances. Steel was a great improvement on iron as it is stronger and some types of steel do not rust as easily. Some of the best steel was made by metal workers in India in 400 BCE. They sealed iron and carbon into clay cubicles and roasted the cubicles in a furnace at very high temperatures to make steel.

Wootz steel
Ancient Indian steel, known as wootz, was famed for its toughness. Metalsmiths hammered out sheets of steel and sharpened their edges to make new, more effective tools and weapons.

STEEL SWORDS

Using high-quality steel, Japanese swordmakers perfected the art of making a sword. The legendary swordsmith Amakuni Yasutsuna is said to have made the first single-edged sword with a curved blade, known as a katana, in around 700 CE. The katana was made using low-carbon steel as its core, with high-carbon steel for the sharp blade. This made the sword very hard to break.

The finished blade has a razor-sharp edge.

1. Before shaping the blade, the metal was hammered out and folded many times. This drew out impurities and ensured an even mix of carbon.

2. High-carbon steel was shaped into a long piece with a U-shaped channel, and a strip of low-carbon steel was fitted into the channel. The two metals were then forged together.

High-carbon steel

Low-carbon steel

1,500°F pre-quenching

70°F post-quenching

3. When the finished sword was pulled from the fire and plunged (quenched) into water, the two different metals contracted at different rates. This created the sword's distinctive curve.

4. Finally, the blade was polished into a fine edge. This process could take several weeks of work.

PLASTIC MATERIALS

From the toothbrush you use to clean your teeth in the morning to the pillows you sleep on at night, you are surrounded by plastics in your everyday life. A plastic material is one that can be molded and pressed into solid shapes. The first synthetic plastics were invented in the 19th century. Since then, many kinds of plastic have been developed.

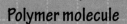

Polymer molecule

WHAT ARE PLASTICS?

Plastics are materials that are made of polymers. These are molecules made from chains of smaller molecules. This structure makes plastics strong and durable materials. Many plastics are also chemically unreactive, which means that they are ideal for making containers. Some plastics become soft when they are heated, then harden as they cool.

Hard as horn, flexible as leather

The first synthetic plastic was invented in 1856 by British chemist Alexander Parkes (1813–1890). It was made using cellulose, a tough material found in the cell walls of plants. The guidebook to the Great Exhibition in London in 1862 said that the new wonder material was "as hard as horn, but as flexible as leather." Parkes' invention was developed to make celluloid, a plastic used to make film for the first movie cameras.

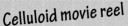

Celluloid movie reel

Bakelite telephone

HEAT-RESISTANT PLASTIC

Celluloid is a highly flammable plastic, meaning that it easily catches fire. In 1909, Belgian chemist Leo Baekeland (1863–1944) invented a heat-resistant plastic called Bakelite, which was made from phenol, a material extracted from coal or petroleum. Lightweight and durable, Bakelite could be moulded into all kinds of shapes and it proved hugely popular.

SYNTHETIC FABRICS

Nylon is a plastic that can be made into thin silklike fibers. These fibers are woven to make fabrics. Nylon was invented in 1935 by American chemist Wallace Hume Carothers (1896–1937). It was first used to make stockings, but is now used for a range of products including waterproof clothing, tents, and seatbelts.

Nylon seatbelt

Kevlar

Kevlar is a plastic material that is five times stronger than steel by weight. It was invented in 1965 by American chemist Stephanie Kwolek (1923–2014). Like nylon, Kevlar can be made into thin fibers that are woven together. The fibers are super-strong due to the ringlike structure of Kevlar molecules. Kevlar is used to make a range of objects, including bulletproof vests and bicycle tires.

Stephanie Kwolek

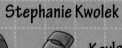

Kevlar bulletproof vest

Bicycle tire

RECYCLING PLASTICS

The durability of synthetic plastics makes them very useful, but causes problems when we dispose of them. Tiny particles called microplastics have polluted the oceans, while burning plastic releases poisonous chemicals. Everybody can help by recycling plastic containers after we have finished using them. This cuts down on waste.

Just 10%

of plastics are currently recycled. We urgently need to increase this amount.

STEAM POWER

The invention of the steam engine in the 18th century marked the start of a series of rapid developments known as the Industrial Revolution. The engines provided a new source of power for a wide variety of industries, from factories to ships and trains.

NEWCOMEN ENGINE

The first practical steam engine was made in 1712 by English inventor Thomas Newcomen (1664–1729). Newcomen's engine worked by pumping a piston up and down inside an open-topped cylinder. It was called an "atmospheric engine" as it made use of air pressure to push the piston down.

Newcomen engines were used to pump water out of mines.

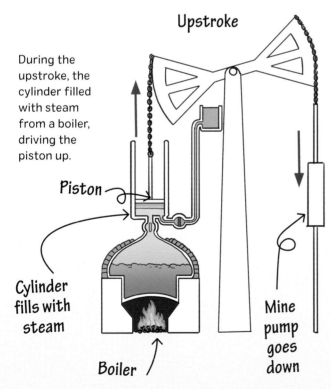

Upstroke

During the upstroke, the cylinder filled with steam from a boiler, driving the piston up.

Piston

Cylinder fills with steam

Boiler

Mine pump goes down

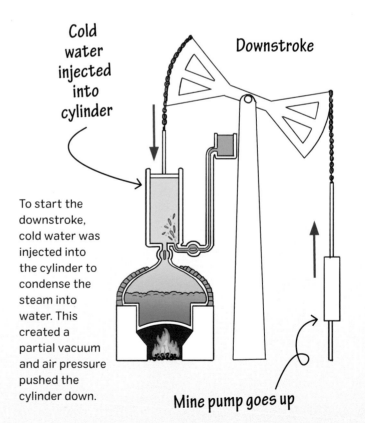

Cold water injected into cylinder

Downstroke

To start the downstroke, cold water was injected into the cylinder to condense the steam into water. This created a partial vacuum and air pressure pushed the cylinder down.

Mine pump goes up

WATT ENGINE

James Watt

In 1764, Scottish inventor James Watt (1736–1839) was repairing a Newcomen engine when he was struck by the amount of energy that was wasted each time the cylinder was cooled. A year later, Watt solved the problem by adding a condenser cylinder next to the power cylinder. At the end of the up stroke, steam was condensed back into water inside the condenser rather than in the power cylinder. This allowed the power cylinder to remain hot all the time.

Watt's new design doubled the efficiency of the steam engine and factories across Britain started using them to power their machines. The Industrial Revolution was now in full swing.

STEAM TRAINS

In 1797, English inventor Richard Trevithick (1771–1833) invented the first high-pressure steam engine. Placing the steam under pressure removed the need for a condenser and allowed the cylinders to be smaller and lighter. For the first time, steam engines could be mounted on vehicles such as trains.

In 1808, Trevithick set up a "Steam Circus" in London to show off his new idea. People paid to watch his train drive around a circular track.

Pacific Railroad

Within a few decades of Trevithick's invention, train tracks were being laid around the world. In the USA, a 1,800-mile track from Iowa to San Francisco was completed in 1869. Known as the Pacific Railroad, the new track connected the east and west coasts of the USA and led to fast economic development in the West.

THE ELECTRIC BATTERY

A battery is a device that turns stored chemical energy into a flow of electricity when it is connected to a circuit. The battery was invented as a result of a scientific disagreement between two Italian physicists.

ANIMAL ELECTRICITY?

In 1787, working with his wife Lucia (1743–1788), Luigi Galvani (1737–1798) demonstrated that a dead frog's legs could be made to twitch by connecting the muscle to an iron wire and the nerve to a copper wire. Galvani thought that they had demonstrated the existence of "animal electricity," a force that powered living things.

VOLTA'S PILE

Galvani's friend and colleague Alessandro Volta (1745–1827) praised Galvani's work, but he disagreed with Galvani's conclusions. According to Volta, the frog's leg was not producing electricity, but merely conducting it. Volta thought that the flow of electricity was produced by the metals Galvani had used as electrodes. He set out to prove his theory by experimenting with different metals. In 1800, these experiments led to the invention of the first electric battery, known as a voltaic pile.

Volta showed his invention to French Emperor Napoleon.

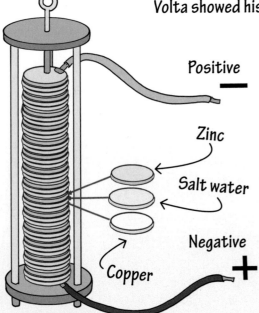

Positive —

Zinc

Salt water

Negative +

Copper

HOW IT WORKED

Volta's pile was made of alternating disks of zinc and copper, separated by cloth soaked in salt water. When the top and bottom disk were connected by a wire, electricity started to flow through the circuit. The taller the pile, the stronger the current of electricity.

Volta did not fully understand the science behind his invention. Scientists later discovered that the salt water plays a crucial role in the voltaic pile. Called an electrolyte, it causes chemical reactions at the metal disks. The zinc electrode dissolves into the water, while hydrogen gas forms around the copper electrode. These reactions cause a flow of electrons through the electrolyte from the zinc to the copper.

RECHARGING BATTERIES

All batteries produce a flow of electrons from chemical reactions. Once the chemicals are used up, the battery goes flat. In rechargeable batteries, such as the batteries inside mobile phones, these reactions are reversed by passing electricity through them.

THE CAMERA

A camera captures an image of a scene.
People have known how to create an image
on a screen for thousands of years, but
it wasn't until the 19th century that
inventors came up with ways to
fix that image forever.

400 BCE Camera obscura

The first written account of a camera obscura ("dark chamber"), or pinhole camera, was made by Chinese philosopher Mozi. He noted how light from an object that passed through a small hole into a dark room created an upside-down image of the object on a wall in the room.

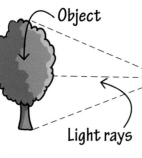

Object

Light rays

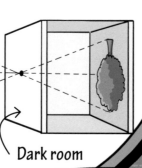

Dark room

1839 Taking portraits

The first commercial camera was invented by French inventor Louis Daguerre (1787–1851). Building on the work of his friend Niépce, Daguerre shortened the exposure time needed for his daguerrotype down to under a minute. With these improvements, portrait photographs became very popular, but the sitter had to remain very still to make a clear image.

A daguerrotype from 1846 is the earliest known photograph of future US president Abraham Lincoln.

1827 First photograph

The first photographs were taken by French inventor Nicéphore Niépce (1765–1833). The oldest surviving image is of the view through the window of Niépce's workshop, taken in 1827. He used an invention that he called the heliograph to fix images in a camera obscura on a plate covered in bitumen. After exposing the plate to sunlight for several hours, he washed the plate, removing only those parts of bitumen that had not been hardened by the light.

1903 First color photos

The French Lumiére Brothers created the first color photos. They invented a process called autochrome that passed light through colored grains of starch. The resulting plates were viewed by shining a light through them.

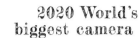

2020 World's biggest camera

The world's most powerful digital camera, the LSST, was built at the SLAC National Accelerator Laboratory in the US. Designed to take photographs of space, the LSST is the size of a small car. It takes images with more than 3 billion pixels. That's enough to make out a golf ball on the ground in a photo taken from a height of 15 miles. You would need 1,500 high-resolution screens to fully display one photo.

15 miles away

Golf ball

1951 High-speed action

US physicist Morton Sultanoff (1920–1970) invented a high-speed camera with a very fast shutter speed. The film was exposed to the light for just 1 millionth of a second. Sultanoff's invention allowed the US Army to capture images of the shock waves caused by explosions.

A high-speed photograph, taken by American inventor Doc Edgerton (1903–1990) in 1964, captures the moment when a playing card is cut in half by a bullet.

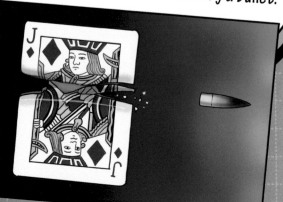

Going digital

Working in the laboratories of camera company Kodak, US inventor Steve Sasson (born 1950) developed the first digital camera. The camera recorded images as a series of numbers on a cassette tape. The first commercial digital camera, the Logitech Fotoman, appeared 16 years later. It created black-and-white images with a resolution of 90,240 pixels (individual dots). Today, the digital cameras in smartphones can capture color images with more than 10 million pixels.

LIGHT BULBS

Today, we take it for granted that we can turn on a light when we enter a room. But before the invention of the incandescent light bulb, most homes were dimly lit by gas or oil lamps.

DEMONSTRATING THE PRINCIPLE

In 1809, British chemist Humphry Davy (1778–1829) invented the arc lamp. Davy showed that a strip of charcoal can be made to glow when an electric current is passed through it. He demonstrated his invention in science lectures, but it was not a practical light bulb. It ran down batteries quickly and the intense heat ate away at the charcoal strips.

Arc lamp →

Davy gave public lectures in packed halls.

Practical bulb

The first practical light bulbs were developed independently in the 1870s by American Thomas Edison and Englishman Joseph Swan. The two men initially disputed the invention but later settled for a joint patent. The bulb worked by passing electricity through a thin carbon filament encased in a glass bulb from which the air had been pumped out. Within a few years, millions of homes across North America and Europe were being fitted with electric lighting.

Prolific inventor

American Thomas Edison (1847–1931) was one of the most prolific inventors in history. In addition to the first commercial light bulb, Edison invented a record player (below) and a movie camera. In total, he filed more than 1,000 patents. Edison was the first inventor to establish a research laboratory, working with a team of scientists and engineers to develop new devices that he could sell to the public.

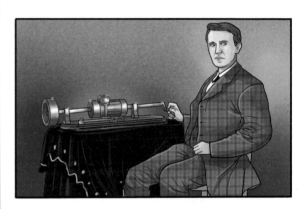

NEW YORK LIGHTS UP

New York City was first lit up by electric lights on September 4, 1882. Before turning on the lights, a power grid of electric cables had to be laid. Once that was done, the Edison Illuminating Company switched on its power station at Pearl Street Station, Manhattan, and thousands of bulbs installed in the buildings around it started to glow.

SAVING ENERGY

While the incandescent light bulb produces a bright light, about 95 percent of the energy passing through it is given off as heat and only 5 percent as light. This makes it very inefficient. Today, we use more efficient light bulbs such as LEDs (Light Emitting Diodes). These bulbs convert nearly 50 percent of the energy passing through them into light. They also last much longer than incandescent light bulbs.

Modern sports stadiums are lit by banks of LED lights.

SENDING MESSAGES

The invention of the telegraph in the 1830s was made possible by advances in our understanding of electricity. Within a few decades, an extensive network of wires covered the globe, providing instant long-distance communication, first by telegraph and later by telephone.

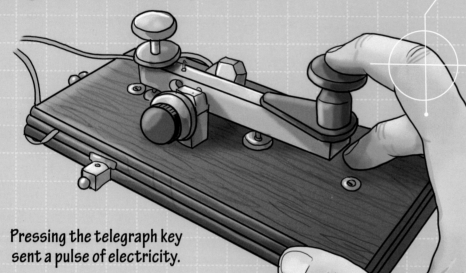

Pressing the telegraph key sent a pulse of electricity.

DOWN THE WIRE

The first practical telegraph system was developed in the 1830s by American Samuel Morse (1791–1872). After Alessandro Volta's invention of the battery in 1800 (see page 21), many inventors had been experimenting with the idea of sending messages using an electric current. Working with mechanic Alfred Vail, Morse developed a telegraph system in which a transmitter sent a pulse of electricity down a wire to a receiver at the other end.

MORSE CODE

To transmit messages using pulses of electricity, Morse and Vail created a code that assigned a set of dots (short pulses) and dashes (long pulses) to each number and letter. They demonstrated their telegraph in 1844 by sending a telegram in Morse Code from Baltimore to Washington, D.C. The message was transmitted along wires suspended from a series of poles.

Morse Code is still used today on ships using signal lamps. The international distress signal in Morse Code is SOS. The letters do not stand for words. They were chosen as they form a simple repeated pattern: dot-dot-dot-dash-dash-dash-dot-dot-dot...

S   O   S

● ● ● ▬ ▬ ▬ ● ● ●

CONNECTING CONTINENTS

In 1858, undersea telegraph cables were laid under the Atlantic Ocean, connecting the USA to the UK. The first message sent along the cables was from US President James Buchanan to British Queen Victoria. The cables broke after three weeks, but new cables were successfully laid eight years later to establish a permanent link between North America and Europe.

The cable is pulled ashore in Canada.

Bell speaking into his telephone.

Transmitting voices

The next big breakthrough came in the 1870s. Scottish inventor Alexander Graham Bell (1847–1922) developed a system that varied the strength of the electric current running along telegraph wires. By doing this, Bell said that he could "telegraph any sound, even speech." Bell spoke the first words along a telephone line in 1876, to his assistant Thomas Watson: "Mr. Watson come here, I want to see you."

The US transcontinental telephone network.

LONG-DISTANCE CALL

A telephone network connecting the East Coast of the US with the West Coast was finished in 1915. It consisted of 14,000 miles of copper wire strung across 130,000 telephone poles. The first call along the network was made from New York to San Francisco. It took 23 minutes for five telephone operators along the line to connect the call.

Fiber-optic cables

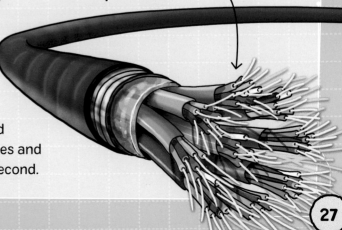

High-speed connections

The final telegraph message was sent in 2013, when India's telegraph service ended 169 years after the first message. Today, the world is connected by high-speed fiber-optic cables, and calls with both images and sound can be connected in a fraction of a second.

27

BROADCASTING TO THE WORLD

Radio broadcasts send messages through the air in the form of radio waves. They transformed communication as signals could be broadcast everywhere at once, not just along a wire.

BROADCASTING MORSE CODE

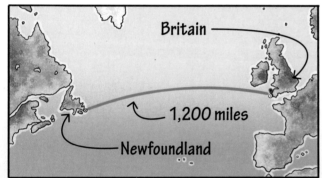

Britain

1,200 miles

Newfoundland

In the 1895, a young Italian inventor called Guglielmo Marconi (1874–1937) invented a way of sending signals using radio waves. Called the wireless telegraph, Marconi's invention allowed Morse Code messages to be sent through the air. He demonstrated the power of his invention in 1901 by sending a signal more than 1,200 miles across the Atlantic from Britain to Newfoundland.

Marconi and his assistants raised the receiving antenna in Newfoundland with the help of a kite.

BROADCASTING SOUNDS

The first voice to be heard on the radio was that of Canadian inventor Reginald Fessenden (1866–1932) in a broadcast in 1906. It was heard by astonished telegraph operators on ships in the Atlantic Ocean. Fessenden developed a system for broadcasting sounds called amplitude modulation (AM). The amplitude, or size, of the wave varied according to the strength of the signal. In this way, radio could broadcast voices and music.

Fessenden in his studio

In 1933, US engineer Edwin Armstrong invented frequency modulation (FM), which broadcasts sounds by varying the frequency of the radio wave. FM broadcasts are much clearer than AM.

AM: Amplitude varies

Signal wave

FM: Frequency varies

LONG OR SHORT WAVES?

The first messages sent by Marconi and Fessenden used long-wave radio. Long-wave, low-frequency radio can be transmitted over long distances because the waves follow the curve of Earth's surface. Long-wave radio transmits sounds using AM. Short-wave, or very high-frequency radio waves (called VHF), can carry FM signals, but these do not curve around Earth's surface. They only travel in straight lines. To send a VHF message a long distance, it must first be sent to a satellite in orbit. The satellite receives the message and transmits it back down to Earth.

Long wave

A   B

Short wave

A   B

High-definition TV signals are broadcast using ultra-high-frequency (UHF) radio waves, which are even shorter than VHF.

MOVING PICTURES

In the late 19th century, as camera technology improved, inventors experimented with ways to make moving pictures. By the 20th century, inventors were looking for ways to send moving pictures via radio waves.

THE FIRST MOVIE

In 1896, the French Lumière Brothers produced the first ever movie—a film of a train pulling into a station. The brothers had invented a camera they called the Cinèmatographe. It operated as both the camera and the projector, playing films at a rate of 16 frames per second. The camera was operated by hand by turning a crank.

The brothers set up their camera on the platform.

Scene from The Trip to the Moon

TELLING STORIES

The first movies were made using one stationary camera, but moviemakers quickly started to use their imagination to tell stories on film. In 1902, French filmmaker Georges Méliès (1861–1938) made the first science fiction film, *The Trip to the Moon*, about a group of astronauts who meet aliens on the Moon. His movies were very popular, and by the 1910s movie studios were opening around the world.

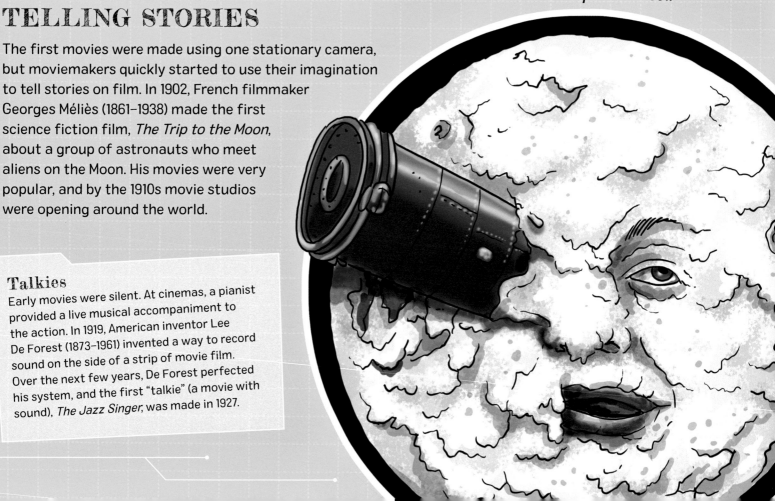

Talkies

Early movies were silent. At cinemas, a pianist provided a live musical accompaniment to the action. In 1919, American inventor Lee De Forest (1873–1961) invented a way to record sound on the side of a strip of movie film. Over the next few years, De Forest perfected his system, and the first "talkie" (a movie with sound), *The Jazz Singer*, was made in 1927.

TELEVISION

The first televisions were developed in the 1920s by American Charles Francis Jenkins (1867–1934) and Scot John Logie Baird (1888–1946). Jenkins sent the first still image via radio waves in 1922, then Baird broadcast the first moving image in 1925. The images were formed of 30 lines that repeated 12 times per second. This made a dim, flickering image, and television was not immediately popular. However, by the 1930s, the technology had improved and regular broadcasts began.

In 1929, Baird built a television camera that sensed invisible infrared radiation. Capable of recording in the dark, the machine was called Noctovisor.

LIVE AND IN COLOR

Color television made color images using combinations of blue, green, and red dots on the screen. The first color broadcast was switched on in the US in 1950, but very few people had color TVs, so it was switched off after a few months. Color television found its first mass audience in 1970 when the soccer World Cup in Mexico was broadcast live and in color in Europe by sending a signal via a satellite.

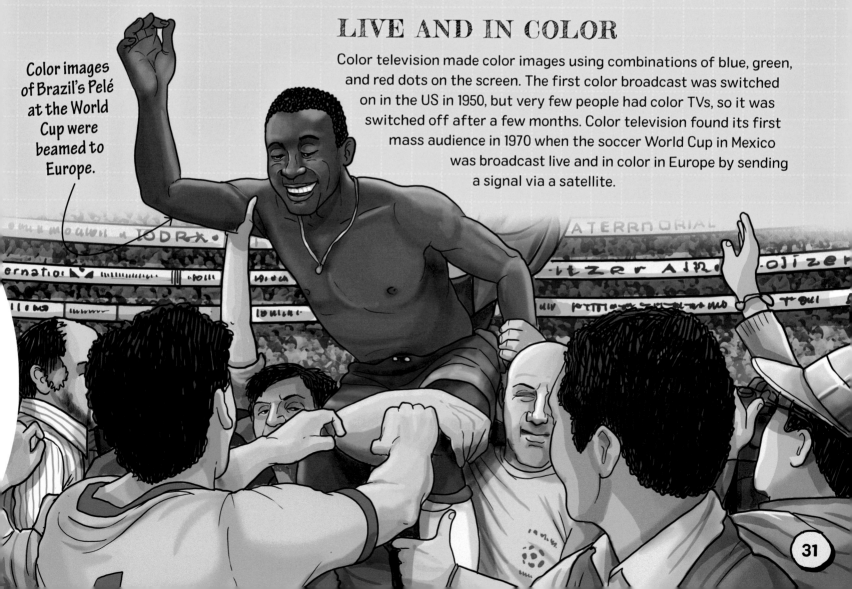

Color images of Brazil's Pelé at the World Cup were beamed to Europe.

TAKING FLIGHT

The first flying machines were unpowered balloons and gliders. Powered heavier-than-air planes were invented at the start of the 20th century. Within a few years, aircraft were making long-distance flights across oceans.

HOT AIR BALLOON

On September 19, 1783, the French Montgolfier brothers, Joseph and Étienne, sent a hot air balloon 2,000 feet into the air above amazed crowds at the Palace of Versailles in Paris. The balloon carried a basket with three passengers: a sheep, a duck, and a chicken. The animals survived their flight, and two months later the first human took to the air in a Montgolfier balloon.

HOW BALLOONS FLOAT

A hot air balloon floats up into the sky because it is lighter than the air around it. The Montgolfiers heated the air inside their balloon with a fire. The hot air expanded, becoming less dense. If the balloon is big enough, the combined density of the balloon, passengers, and hot air becomes less than the density of the atmosphere, and it starts to rise. The pilot controls the flight by adjusting the heat of the air in the balloon.

+212°F

CLIMBING
(lift greater than weight)

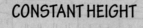

CONSTANT HEIGHT
(lift equal to weight)

+203°F

DESCENDING
(lift less than weight)

+194°F

HEAVIER-THAN-AIR

Orville piloted the first flight, with Wilbur running alongside.

The first powered heavier-than-air flight was made on December 17, 1903 by the American brothers, Wilbur and Orville Wright. Following experiments with unpowered gliders, the brothers designed the Wright Flyer, a biplane powered by a pair of propellers attached to a gasoline engine. They made four flights in total. On the final flight, they covered a distance of 850 feet, but the plane was damaged on landing and it never flew again. A year later, they flew a second plane, the Wright Flyer II, which covered a distance of 5 miles. The age of powered flight had truly taken off.

Air deflected down

Thrust

Lift

Drag

Air deflected down

HOW PLANES FLY

As an aircraft moves forward, its wings generate an upward force called lift, due to the way that they deflect the air passing around them. If the lift is greater than the plane's weight, it rises into the air.

ROCKETS INTO SPACE

In the first half of the 20th century, three inventors working in different countries all dreamed of sending a rocket into space. Their ideas were ridiculed by many people, but they proved their doubters wrong, and the first rocket entered space in 1944.

FIRE ARROWS

The first rockets were powered by gunpowder. This is an explosive chemical mix of sulfur, carbon, and saltpeter, which was invented in China around the 8th century CE. The Chinese filled tubes with gunpowder. Arrows attached to the tubes made the first rocket-powered weapons.

One end of the tube was sealed.

As the gunpowder burned, hot gas escaped from the open end.

RUSSIAN VISIONARY

Russian schoolteacher Konstantin Tsiolkovsky (1857-1935) imagined sending humans into space. Tsiolkovsky studied the mathematics of space travel and calculated that rockets would need to reach a velocity of 26,000 feet per second to enter orbit around Earth. He drew a design for a rocket fueled by liquid hydrogen and liquid oxygen.

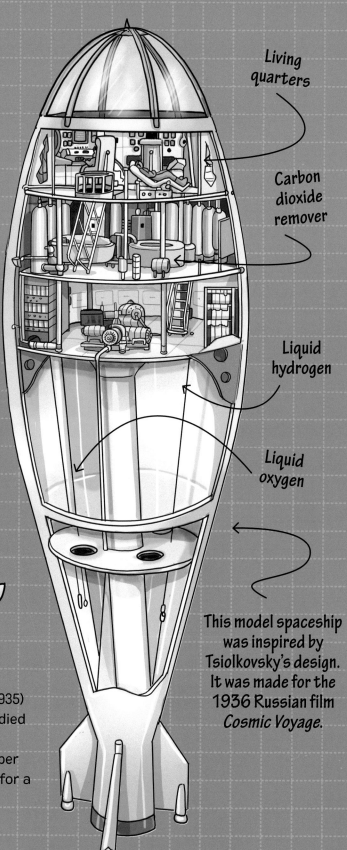

Living quarters

Carbon dioxide remover

Liquid hydrogen

Liquid oxygen

This model spaceship was inspired by Tsiolkovsky's design. It was made for the 1936 Russian film *Cosmic Voyage*.

SUCCESSFUL LAUNCHES

American physicist Robert Goddard (1882–1945) worked on similar ideas to Tsiolkovsky, designing multi-stage rockets powered by liquid fuel. His first successful flight with liquid fuel came in 1926, when he sent a rocket powered by liquid oxygen and gasoline to a height of 40 feet. By 1937, he was building rockets that could reach heights of over 8,000 feet during a 22-second flight.

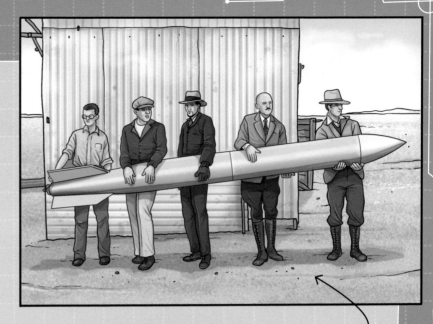

Goddard (second-right) and four assistants hold his rocket.

REACHING SPACE

Working in Germany, Romanian rocketeer Hermann Oberth (1894–1989) wrote a book on the possibilities of space flight, which inspired the formation of rocketeer societies across Germany. Oberth developed the first rocket-powered plane in 1929. Later, he worked with a team of rocketeers to develop long-range missiles. This led to the development of the V-2 missile (right), which became the first manmade object to enter space in 1944, reaching up to 110 miles before falling back to Earth.

SLS

is designed to launch missions to the Moon.

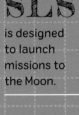

WORLD'S LARGEST ROCKET

Developed to launch manned missions to the Moon, NASA's Space Launch System (SLS) is the most powerful rocket ever built. Its huge tanks hold 740,000 gallons of liquid hydrogen and oxygen. The fuel burns out completely in just 8.5 minutes.

COMPUTERS

Today, we carry computers in our pockets as smartphones, which allow us to connect with people all over the world via the Internet. The world's first computers were the size of a room and operated at much slower speeds than modern computers. Progress has been very fast, with many new inventions along the way.

1953

American computer scientist Grace Hopper (1906–1992) developed the first computer programming language, which was later known as COBOL. Hopper helped to develop the UNIVAC electronic computing systems that were used by NASA to communicate with the astronauts on the Apollo Moon missions of the 1960s and 1970s.

1822

British mathematician Charles Babbage (1791–1871) made a design for the first mechanical computer, which he called a Difference Engine. It would make calculations using a series of rotating metal wheels. Babbage later invented a machine called an Analytical Engine, which was the first design for a programmable computer. Babbage's designs were complex, and they proved too difficult to make in his lifetime.

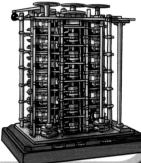

1941

Working independently from Turing, German inventor Konrad Zuse (1910–1995) built the first fully programmable computer, the Z3. It could perform up to 10 operations per second. Today's computers perform billions of operations per second. The Z3 was destroyed during a bombing raid in World War II, but Zuse made a functioning replica in 1961.

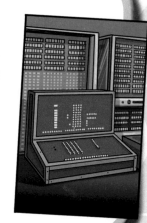

1843

British mathematician Ada Lovelace (1815–1852) wrote a series of notes about Babbage's Analytical Engine. In her notes, Lovelace detailed a program designed to calculate a sequence of numbers, which may have been the first ever computer program. Lovelace was the first person to see the potential of computers beyond mathematics, suggesting that they could be programmed to perform a wide range of tasks, such as composing music.

1936

British mathematician Alan Turing (1912–1954) described a machine that was capable of making all kinds of computations by running different programs. Called the Universal Turing Machine, the idea provided the basis for all modern computers.

1958

American physicists Jack Kilby and Robert Noyce invented the integrated circuit, also known as a computer chip, which greatly increased computer processing speeds.

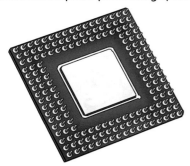

1981

IBM released the Acorn, the first personal computer. It ran on Microsoft's MS-DOS operating system, which later developed into Windows.

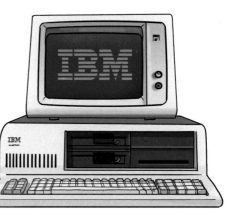

2019

IBM built Q System One, the first quantum computer designed for commercial use. The computer makes calculations using 20 quantum bits, or qubits, which are placed in a special state called a quantum superposition to perform super-fast calculations. Researchers hope that quantum computers will one day become vastly more powerful than today's digital computers.

1989

While working for CERN, the European Organisation for Nuclear Research, British computer scientist Tim Berners-Lee (born 1955) created the World Wide Web (WWW) to allow researchers to share information with each other. Berners-Lee made the first website in 1991. In 1993, CERN made the WWW software freely available to everyone in the world, marking the birth of the modern Internet.

2022

OpenAI released ChatGPT, an artificial intelligence (AI) chatbot that answers questions with human-like text. ChatGPT uses a form of technology called a Large Language Model, which allows a computer to learn for itself. In the future, AI applications like this may do many jobs currently performed by people.

ROBOTS

Robots are machines that can work on their own. Large industrial robots are used on assembly lines in thousands of factories, manufacturing products from cars to medicines. Today, smaller robots are being developed to carry out a range of tasks, even pollinating plants.

PERFORMING ARM

In 1966, US television audiences were wowed by the tricks of a robotic arm called Unimate, which performed tricks such as playing golf and conducting music. Unimate was the world's first industrial robot. It was created in 1956 by American inventor George Devol (1912–2011) and first went into use on a General Motors (GM) automobile assembly line in 1961. GM opened a new robotic assembly line fitted with Unimate robot welders in 1969. It could make 100 cars per hour, more than twice the speed of factories with human welders.

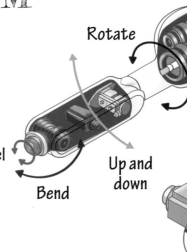

Rotate

Swivel

Bend

Up and down

Backward and forward

Revolve

Robots can work more quickly and accurately than humans, make fewer mistakes, and never get tired or distracted.

ROBOTIC SURGERY

Some surgeons use robots to help them during operations. The surgeon controls a mechanical arm from a computer. A camera on the robot allows the surgeon to guide it to exactly the right place.

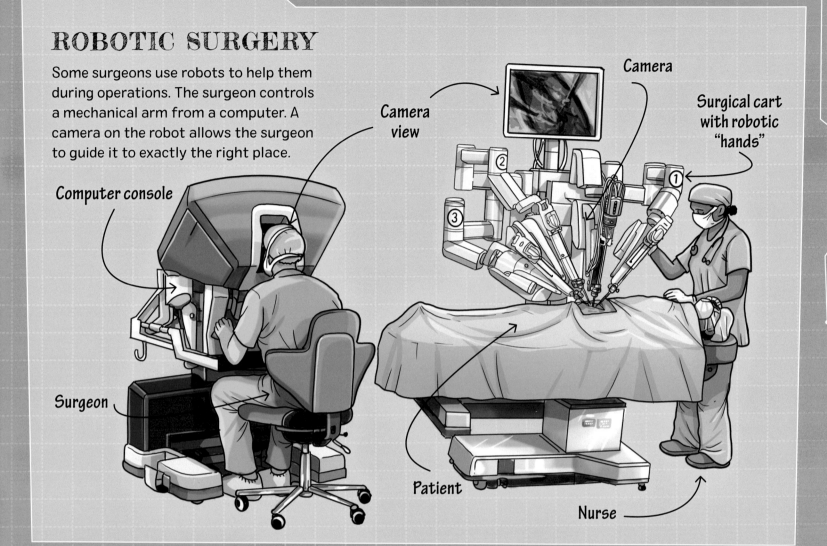

Computer console

Camera view

Camera

Surgical cart with robotic "hands"

Surgeon

Patient

Nurse

ROBOBEES

The size of a small paperclip and weighing less than 1/10 gram, RoboBees are the invention of scientists at Harvard University in the USA. These microrobots flap their wings 120 times per second using artificial muscles. They are fitted with sensors that mimic the senses of bees, allowing them to navigate their way through the skies. The scientists hope to use RoboBees for crop pollination and to assist on search-and-rescue missions.

SEEING THE INVISIBLE

Microscopes magnify images, revealing objects that are invisible to the naked eye. Modern microscopes even allow us to see individual atoms. Scanners allow us to see inside living bodies, revealing the structures under the skin.

1895

German physicist Wilhelm Röntgen (1845–1923) took the first radiograph image, of his wife Anna Bertha's hand. The image revealed the bones under the skin using high-energy X-rays. Röntgen had discovered X-rays by accident during an experiment a few weeks earlier.

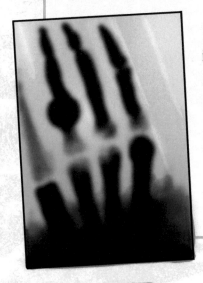

In the X-ray image of her hand, Anna Bertha is wearing a ring on one finger.

1600

Dutch eyeglasses-maker Zacharias Jansen (1585–c.1632) may have invented the first microscope, using two lenses to magnify images about 20 times.

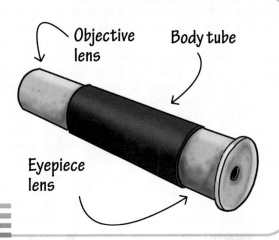

Objective lens

Body tube

Eyepiece lens

1660s

The first book of drawings made using a microscope was published by English scientist Robert Hooke (1635–1703). His drawings included a detailed study of a flea.

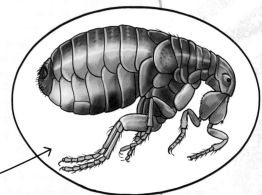

Dutchman Antonie van Leeuwenhoek (1632–1723) ground his own lenses to magnify images 200 times. Van Leeuwenhoek discovered microbes that he called "animalcules" (tiny animals). He was also the first person to describe red blood cells, which are less than 0.01 millimeters across.

1826

British physicist Joseph Lister (1786–1869) developed a microscope that combined a series of weaker lenses to give much clearer images. Using these improved microscopes, German scientists Mathias Schleiden and Theodor Schwann drew the internal structures of animal and plant cells.

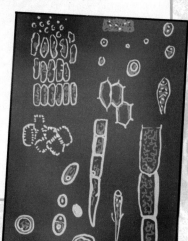

1938

German scientists Ernst Ruska (1906–1988) and Max Knoll (1897–1969) made the first electron microscope. Rather than using light, an electron microscope fires a beam of electrons through an object. A lens magnifies the image, which becomes visible on a screen at the base of the microscope. The best magnification a light microscope can achieve is 1,400 times. An electron microscope can magnify an image by up to 500,000 times to reveal the complex structures of tiny objects such as viruses.

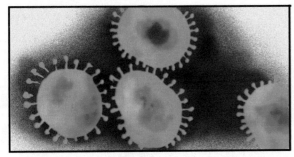

Coronaviruses were first seen through an electron microscope by Scottish virologist June Almeida in 1964.

1971

American chemist Paul Lauterbur (1929–2007) developed a new technique for looking at soft tissues inside bodies using electromagnetism. This led to the development of Magnetic Resonance Imaging (MRI). Doctors use MRI scanners to examine soft body parts such as brains.

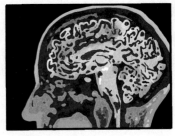

MRI scans reveal complex structures in the brain.

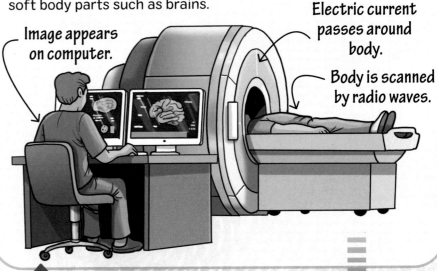

Image appears on computer.

Electric current passes around body.

Body is scanned by radio waves.

1949

British physicist John Wild (1914–2009) headed a group that developed the use of ultrasound to produce images of the insides of bodies. Ultrasounds are sounds with a very high frequency that we cannot hear. Today, doctors use ultrasound as a safe way to produce images of fetuses developing inside their mother's womb.

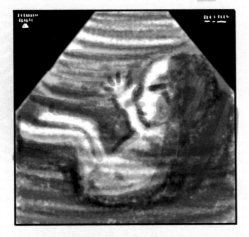

Doctors can check the health of a fetus inside its mother's womb using ultrasound.

1981

The scanning tunneling microscope (STM) was developed by German Gerd Binning (born 1947) and Swiss Heinrich Rohrer (1933–2013). Rather than using beams of light or electrons, an STM runs an extremely sharp tip over the surface of objects. STMs allow scientists to produce images of individual atoms.

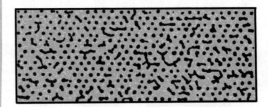

Seen through an STM, gold atoms are revealed to organize themselves into a honeycomb-like structure.

FAILED INVENTIONS

Most inventors have more failures than successes. These are a few of the inventions that have failed to change the way we live.

ELECTRIC PEN

Not all of Thomas Edison's inventions changed the world. In 1875, he invented an electric pen that could be used to copy documents. The pen required a lot of maintenance and did not sell well. However, Edison's idea later inspired American tattoo artist Samuel O'Reilly (1854–1909) to create the first electric tattoo machine.

Needle moved rapidly up and down.

Electric motor

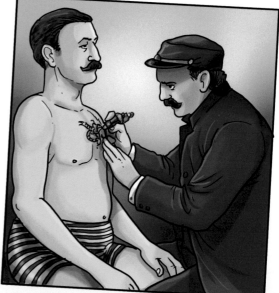

The needle was adapted for puncturing skin to make tattoos.

READING MACHINE

In 1922, US Admiral Bradley Fiske (1854–1942) invented a reading machine that he thought would mean the end of books. The Fiske Reading Machine allowed readers to read a book printed in tiny letters by holding a magnifying glass up to their eyes. Fiske's invention was sold as a great way to save paper and space. But it turned out that people didn't like having to hold a lens up to their eyes for hours at a time.

CINERAMA

In the 1950s, the movie industry felt under threat from the spread of television. Invented by American Fred Waller (1886–1954), Cinerama was a new moviegoing experience with a huge, curved screen to make the viewer feel like they were completely surrounded. Films were shown using three projectors pointing at different angles. Cinerama proved popular with audiences, but it was an expensive process and it never caught on. Today's moviegoers gain a similar experience at IMAX cinemas.

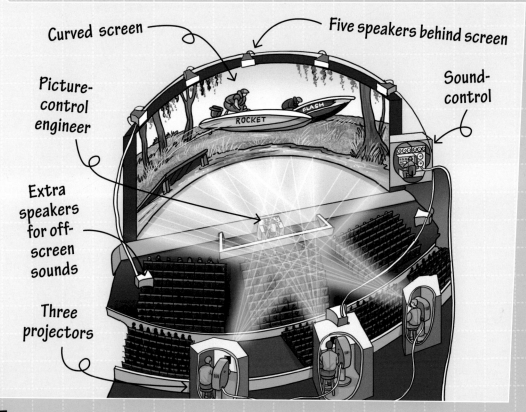

Curved screen

Five speakers behind screen

Sound-control

Picture-control engineer

Extra speakers for off-screen sounds

Three projectors

Spy glasses

Google launched Google Glass in 2014. These were smart glasses fitted with a computer. The wearer could control a display screen using their voice, and the glasses could take photos or record video of what they were seeing. Labeled "spy glasses," they were banned from many public places, including cinemas and casinos, and Google withdrew them from sale after just one year.

WORST INVENTOR EVER?

American inventor Thomas Midgely (1889–1944) came up with two of the worst ideas of the 20th century. In the 1920s, Midgely devised a way to make gasoline for cars burn more efficiently by adding lead to it. This caused pollution that was linked to health problems in children. In the 1930s, he developed gases called CFCs for use in refrigerators and aerosol sprays. It was later discovered that CFCs destroy the ozone layer high in the atmosphere, which protects us from harmful ultraviolet light. Both leaded gasoline and CFC sprays have now been banned.

FUTURE INVENTIONS

Inventors around the world are working hard on the next big ideas that could change our lives. These are a few that are in development.

Launch tube

SPACE CATAPULT

The satellites of the future could be launched into orbit by a catapult. SpinLaunch is a prototype system that spins a payload inside a giant drum. The payload reaches a speed of 5,000 mph before it is shot out into space through a launch tube.

Satellite spins inside vacuum-sealed drum.

Special film mimics eye muscles.

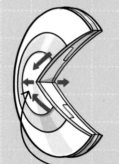

Bionic eye
Scientists at the University of California have developed a contact lens that is fitted with a zoom. The wearer gives the signal by blinking twice and the lens gives them an instant zoomed-in image.

Shape of lens is changed by electrical signal from blinking.

SMART SKELETON

Exoskeletons are robotic frames that are fitted over your body to help you move. In the future, exoskeletons could be linked up to people's brains to allow them to control the movements with their thoughts. People with disabilities who are currently confined to wheelchairs may be able to walk again.

NANOBOTS

Nanobots are microscopic robots that are just a few millionths of a meter long. In the future, nanobots could be sent into people's bodies to deliver drugs to just the right place, or even to carry out surgery and repair damaged organs.

Nanobots will swim through the bloodstream.

Red blood cells

Liquid trees

Serbian scientists have invented a new way to clean the air in cities. Called LIQUID 3, it is a tank filled with water and algae. Like trees, the algae take carbon dioxide from the air and release oxygen during a process called photosynthesis. These small green tanks could make for cleaner air and help to fight global warming.

Vatajankoski

POLAR NIGHT ENERGY

JL METALS

Sand battery

Not all the inventions of the future will be high-tech. Finnish engineers have invented a low-tech solution to the problem of storing energy from renewable sources such as solar or wind power. Sand is packed into a container. The sand is heated up by air that has been warmed by passing an electric current through it. The sand stays hot for a long time and provides heating for local homes.

GLOSSARY

Alloy
A metal made by mixing together two or more metals or a metal and another substance such as carbon.

Bitumen
A sticky black substance made from oil.

Chemistry
The study of the properties of substances and the way they react with one another.

Condense
To change from a gas into a liquid, such as when steam changes into liquid water.

Density
A measure of the mass of a substance or object per unit volume.

Digital
Stored in electronic form as a series of 0s and 1s.

Electrode
A conductor through which an electric current enters or leaves a substance.

Electromagnetism
A force that occurs between electrically charged particles. The force produces electricity and magnetism. Electromagnetic waves such as light waves carry energy from one place to another.

Electron
A tiny subatomic particle that has negative electrical charge. Electricity is a flow of electrons.

Fiber-optic cable
A cable made of flexible glass fibers through which signals can be sent at high speed in the form of light.

Filament
A thin, threadlike wire made of a substance with a high melting point. When electricity is passed through a filament in an incandescent light bulb, the filament glows.

LCD
Short for Liquid Crystal Display. A screen that displays images using liquid crystals that become visible when electricity is passed through them.

LED
Short for Light-Emitting Diode. A device that glows when electricity is passed through it.

Lift
A force that pushes an object such as an airplane upward as it moves forward.

Molecule
A group of atoms that are bound together to form the smallest unit of a chemical.

Operation
In computers, the result of the processing of a single instruction.

Payload
An object, such as a satellite or a space probe, carried into space by a rocket.

Piston
A disk that moves up and down inside a cylinder in an engine, providing the engine with its power.

Pixel
The smallest unit on a digital display screen. The more pixels the screen has, the sharper the image.

Radio wave
A low-energy electromagnetic wave with a long wavelength.

Seismograph
An instrument that detects earthquakes.

Syllable
A unit of speech containing a vowel sound and one or more consonant sounds. Depending on the language, words are often made up of several syllables.

Synthetic
A substance made artificially using a chemical reaction.

Telegram
A message sent along a telegraph wire.

Typesetter
A worker whose job it is to arrange the blocks in a printing press.

Velocity
An object's speed in a particular direction.

X-ray
A high-energy electromagnetic wave with a very short wavelength.

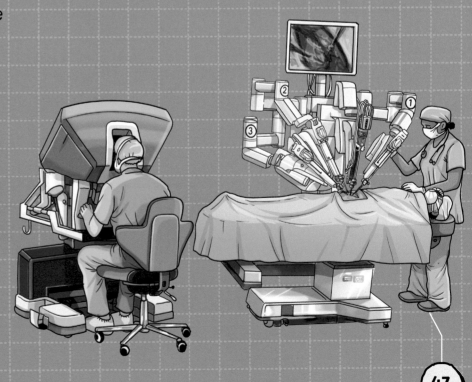

INDEX